To
Christopher and Anne
who give great joy

compiled by Margaret Donald v. Schaack

Published by The C. R. Gibson Company, Norwalk, Connecticut

Joy of Man

See golden days, fruitful of golden deeds,
With Joy and Love triumphing.
John Milton

Man's joy is a deep and abiding condition which he has to
dig beneath the surface to find. The pools of pleasure soon
dry up, but the well of joy is bottomless.

Charles Shaw

Creative spirit, by whose aid
The world's foundations first were laid,
Come, visit every pious mind,
Come, pour Thy joy on humankind.

Charlemagne

The charitable man is loved by all. His friendship is prized highly; his heart is at rest and full of joy, for he suffers not from repentance; he receives the opening flow of his reward and the fruit that ripens from it. Hard it is to understand: By giving away food, we get more strength; by bestowing clothing on others, we gain more beauty; by donating abodes of purity and truth, we acquire great treasures.

Buddha

Little joys refresh us constantly, like house bread, and never bring disgust: and great ones, like sugar-bread briefly, and, then satisfy.

Johann Paul Richter

There is ever a song somewhere, my dear,
   Be the skies above dark or fair.
There is ever a song that our hearts may
   hear —
There is ever a song somewhere, my dear,
There is ever a song somewhere.

James Whitcomb Riley

Mere longevity is a good thing for those who watch life from the sidelines. For those who play the game, an hour may be a year, a single day's work an achievement for eternity.

Gabriel Heatter

A string of excited, fugitive, miscellaneous pleasures is not joy. Joy resides in imaginative reflection and judgment, when the picture of one's life, or of human life, as it truly has been or is. It satisfies the will, and is gladly accepted.

George Santayana

All who joy would win
Must share it —
Happiness was born
A twin.

George Gordon, Lord Byron

Joy is a constituent of life, a necessity of life; it is an element of life's value and life's power. As every man has need of joy, so too, every man has a right to joy. . . . It is a condition of religious living.

Paul Wilhelm von Keppler

. . . let us eat, and be merry.

Luke 15:23

We cannot assemble our joys, but we can absorb them as they succeed one another. Our happiness is the adjustment of man to his world, of the inner life to its outer existence.

Charles Shaw

Eat with the Rich, but go to the play with the Poor, who are capable of Joy.

Logan Pearsall Smith

Man's real life is happy, chiefly because he is ever expecting that it soon will be.

Edgar Allen Poe

Seek to convince us of the eternal joy of existence. We seek this joy in phenomena, but behind phenomena. We are to perceive how all that comes into being. We are really for brief moments, primordial being itself, and feel its indomitable desire for being and joy in existence.

Friedrich Wilhelm Nietzsche

The true joy of man is in doing that which is most proper to his nature; and the first property of man is to be kindly affected towards them that are of one kind with himself.

Marcus Aurelius

Happiness is not found, it is made. One can only give the seed of happiness to another. Each one must make it grow within himself.

Marciso Irala

I have drunk deep of joy,
And I will taste no other wine tonight.
Percy Bysshe Shelley

If I meet people to whom it is possible to open oneself out as a man who thinks, I feel a passionate enjoyment in their society as if I were as young as ever. If I stumble on a young man who is ready for serious discussion, I give myself up to a joyous exchange which makes the difference between our ages a thing of no account.
Albert Schweitzer

Man is the artificer of his own happiness.
Henry David Thoreau

How good is man's life, the mere living!
how fit to employ
All the heart and the soul and the
senses forever in joy!
Robert Browning

A positive thing: in Joy one does not only feel secure, but something goes out from one's self to the universe, a warm, possessive effluence of love.
John Buchan

9

When the power of imparting joy is equal to the will — the human soul requires no other heaven.

Percy Bysshe Shelley

Our actions are necessarily determined by that which affords us the greatest pleasure.

St. Augustine

Thanks to the human heart by which
we live,
Thanks to its tenderness, its joys, and
fears,
To me the meanest flower that blows
can give
Thoughts that do often lie too deep for
tears.

William Wordsworth

Gladness of heart is the very life of man,
cheerfulness prolongs his days.

Ecclesiasticus 30:22

Joy is a flame which association alone can keep alive, and which goes out unless communicated.

Alphonse de Lamartine

Joy of Nature

The delicious soft spring suggesting air
How it fills my veins with life!
Henry David Thoreau

Joyousness is Nature's garb of health.
Alphonse de Lamartine

Worship all ye that lovers be, this May,
    For all your bliss the kalends are begun,
And sing with us: Away, winter, away,
    Come, summer, come, the sweet season and sun.
The quickening breath of May
Melts all nature into ecstasy and song.
James I of Scotland

11

The joyous Book of Spring
Lies open, writ in blossoms.
William Allingham

The sun does not shine for a few trees and flowers, but for the wide world's joy.
Henry Ward Beecher

Came voices of the well-contented doves;
The lark could scarce get out his notes for joy
And shout his song together as he near'd
His happy home.
Alfred, Lord Tennyson

'Tis a little thing to give a cup of water; yet its draught of cool refreshment, drained by fevered lips, may give a shock of pleasure to the frame more exquisite than when nectarean juice renews the life of joy in happiest hours.
Sir Thomas Talfourd

Joy is the mainspring in the whole
Of endless Nature's calm rotation.
Joy moves the dazzling wheels that roll
In the great timepiece of creation.
Johann von Schiller

Yes, in the poor man's garden grow
Far more than herbs and flowers —
Kind thoughts, contentment, peace of mind
And joy for weary hours.

Mary Howitt

The wisest, happiest of our kind are they
That ever walk content in Nature's way.
God's goodness, measuring as it may,
For whom the gravest thought of what they miss
Chastening the fullness of a present bliss.

William Wordsworth

How sweet to be a cloud
Floating in the blue,
Every little cloud
Always sings aloud.

A. A. Milne

What is joy? A sunbeam between two clouds.

Mme. Deluzy

Memory brings us joys faint as is the perfume of the flowers,
faded and dried, of the summer that is gone.

Henry Ward Beecher

God shall hold His World above despair
Look to the east —
Where up in the lucid sky
The morning climbs!
The day shall yet be fair.

Charles Thaxter

Surely joy is the condition of life. Think of the young frogs
that leap in ponds, the myriads of insects ushered into being
on a summer evening, the incessant note of the hyla with
which the woods ring in the Spring — the nonchalance of
the butterfly carrying change painted in a thousand colours
upon its wing — or the brook minnow stoutly stemming the
current whose luster of scales worn bright are reflected upon
the bank. For joy I could embrace the earth.

Henry David Thoreau

I saw far flung mountains risen,
From abysmal darkness like prisms
Only you God, witnessed
Joy break out in birds and beasts.

Is it joy
Is it grief
Stirring my spirit this night
Like moonlight?

Father Leonardos Andrickus

14

Winter has a joy for me
    While the Seasons' charms I read.
Lowly, meek, from blemish free
    In the snowdrop's pensive head.

Spring returns and brings along
    Life invigorating suns
Hark, the turtle's plaintive song
    Seems to speak his dying groans.

Summer has a thousand charms
    All expressive of his worth,
'Tis his sun that lights and warms
    His air that cools the earth.

What! Has autumn left to say
    Nothing of a Saviour's grace?
Yet, the beams of a milder day
    Tell me of His smiling face.

William Cowper

Seas roll to waft me, suns to light me rise;
My footstool Earth, my canopy the skies!

Alexander Pope

A thing of beauty is a joy for ever.

John Keats

15

Life answering life, across the vast profound,
By common grace.
I think this sudden joyousness
    which illumes
Far more than herbs and flowers
Kind thoughts, contentment, peace of mind
    and joy for weary bones.
Mary Howitt

Sing out my soul, thy songs of joy;
    Such as happy bird will sing,
Beneath a Rainbow's lovely arch,
    In early spring.
W. H. Davies

I chatter, chatter, as I flow
    To join the brimming river,
For men may come and men may go,
    But I go on forever.
Alfred, Lord Tennyson

These are flowers that fly and all but sing.
And now, from having ridden out desire
They lie, closed over, in the wind and cling
Where wheels have freshly sliced the April mire.
Robert Frost

Joy of Life

Praise they that will times past, I joy to see
My self now live: this age best pleaseth me.
Robert Herrick

He is the rich man, and enjoys the fruits of riches, who summer and winter forever can find delight in his own thought.
Henry David Thoreau

Although joy, like everything else, can be experienced only
in particular moments, it is found in conceiving the total
issue and the ultimate fruits of life; and no passing sensation
could be enjoyed with a free mind, unless the blessing of
reason and of a sustained happiness were felt to hang over it.
George Santayana

17

There is the laughter which is born out of the pure joy of living, the spontaneous expression of health and energy — the sweet laughter of the child. This is a gift of God.

J. E. Bodin

My mind to me a kingdom is;
    Such present joys therein I find
That it excels all other bliss
    That earth affords or grows by kind:
Though much I want which most
    would have,
Yet still my mind forbids to crave.

Sir Edward Dyer

Good cheer is one of the greatest pleasures of life.

Blaise Pascal

We have lived not in proportion to the number of years that we have spent on the earth, but in proportion as we have enjoyed.

Henry David Thoreau

The happiness habit is developed by simply practicing happy thinking, humor, joy.

Norman Vincent Peale

He that is of a merry heart hath a continual feast.
Proverbs 15:15

I am grateful for what I am and have. My thanksgiving is perpetual. It is surprising how contented one can be with nothing definite — only a sense of existence. My breath is sweet to me. O, how I laugh when I think of my vague indefinite riches. No run on my bank can drain it, for my wealth is not possession but enjoyment.
Henri Rousseau

A man's work is a joy and possession forever.
William Shakespeare

Joy is the sweet voice, Joy the luminous
    cloud —
We in ourselves rejoice!
And thence flows all that charms or ear
    or sight,
All melodies the echoes of that voice,
All colors a suffusion from that light.
Samuel Taylor Coleridge

Work is nature's physician and is essential to human joy.
Galen

19

Happiness lies not in the mere possession of money; it lies in the enjoyment of achievement, in the thrill of creative effort.

Franklin Delano Roosevelt

Be it jewel or toy,
  Not the prize gives the joy,
    But the striving to win the prize.

Pisistratus Caxton

Happiness does not lie in happiness, but in the achievement of it.

Fyodor Dostoevsky

Thou shalt ever joy at eventide if thou spend the day fruitfully.

Thomas à Kempis

Truths that wake,
To perish never:
Which neither listlessness, nor mad endeavour,
    Nor Man nor Boy,
Nor all that is at enmity with joy,
Can utterly abolish or destroy!

Then sing, ye birds, sing, sing a joyous song!

William Wordsworth

Joy in one's work is the consummate tool.

Phillips Brooks

My greatest inspiration is a challenge to attempt the impossible.

Albert A. Michelson

Today, whatever may annoy,
The word for me is Joy, just simple Joy.
Whatever there be of sorrow,
I'll put off till tomorrow.
And when Tomorrow comes, why then
It will be Today and Joy again.

John Kendrick Bangs

Joy is contagious. It can spread like wildfire and wipe the worry from people's minds and keep your thoughts ready for positive action.

Quiet happiness is also catching, when a person quietly gives another enjoyment he makes the other person glad he's alive. He turns worry to joy and hate to love.

Maxwell Maltz

Youth will never live to age unless they keep themselves in health with exercise, and in heart with joyfulness.

Sir Philip Sidney

Human felicity is produced not so much by great pieces of good fortune that seldom happen, as by little advantages that occur every day.

Benjamin Franklin

And the night shall be filled with music,
And the cares, that infest the day,
Shall fold their tents, like the Arabs,
And as silently steal away.

Henry Wadsworth Longfellow

Happiness makes up for height in what it lacks in length.

Robert Frost

Without kindness, there can be no true joy.

Thomas Carlyle

Shall we not then be glad and rejoice in the joy of our children?

Henry Wadsworth Longfellow

Man is a human being who wants to go at life wholeheartedly and enjoy it. In his quest of happiness he wants more than clear ideas and forceful motives, he wants successful emotions.

Anonymous

22

Happy the man, of mortals hap-
    piest he,
Whose quiet mind from vain de-
    sires is free;
Whom neither hopes deceive, nor
    fears torment,
But lives at peace, within himself
    content.

George Granville

The babe by its mother
        Lies bathed in joy
Glide its hours uncounted,
        The sun is its toy;
Shines the peace of all being,
        Without cloud, in its eyes;
And the sum of the world
        In soft miniature lies.

Ralph Waldo Emerson

To aid thy mind's development, — to watch
Thy dawn of little joys, — to sit and see
Almost thy very growth, — to view thee catch
Knowledge of objects, — wonders yet to thee!
To hold thee lightly on a gentle knee,
And print on thy soft cheek a parent's kiss.

George Gordon, Lord Byron

If solid happiness we prize,
Within our breast this jewel lies,
    And they are fools who roam —
The world has nothing to bestow
From our own selves, our joys must flow,
    And that dear hut — our Home.

Nathaniel Cotton

She pictured to herself how this same little sister would in the after time, be herself a grown woman.

    How would she keep, through all her riper years, the simple and loving heart of her childhood? How she would gather about her other little children and make their eyes bright and eager with many a strange tale, perhaps even with the dream of Wonderland of long ago. How would she feel with all their simple sorrows and find a pleasure in all their simple joys, remembering her own child life and the happy summer days.

Lewis Carroll

How small, of all that human hearts endure,
That part which laws or kings can cause or cure!
Still to ourselves in every place consigned,
Our own felicity we make or find:
With secret course, which no loud storms annoy,
Glides the smooth currents of domestic joy.

Samuel Johnson

There's a bliss beyond all that the minstrel has told,
    When two, that are link'd in one heavenly tie,
With heart never changing, and brow never cold,
    Love on thro' all ills, and love on till they die.
One hour of all passion so sacred is worth
    Whole ages of heartless and wandering bliss;
And oh! if there be an Elysium on earth,
    It is this . . . it is this!

Thomas Moore

Joy, Temperance and Repose
Slam the door on the doctor's nose

Friedrich von Logau

Joy is a partnership,
    Grief weeps alone;
Many guests had Cana,
    Gethsemane had one.

Frederic Lawrence Knowles

Your success and happiness lie in you. External conditions
are the accidents of life. The great enduring realities are love
and service. Joy is the holy fire that keeps our purpose warm
and our intelligence aglow. Resolve to keep happy and your
joy in you shall form an invincible host against difficulty.

Helen Keller

Base envy withers at another's joy.

James Thompson

These things have I spoken unto you,
that my joy remain in you, and that
your joy may be fulfilled. This is
my commandment, That ye love one another,
even as I have loved you.

John 15:11

What sunshine is to flowers, smiles are to humanity. They are
but trifles, but scattered along life's pathway the good they do
is inconceivable.

Joseph Addison

The world is a looking-glass, and it gives back to every man
the reflection of his own face. Laugh at it and with it — and
it is a jolly, kind companion.

William Makepeace Thackeray

There's a joy without canker or cark,
There's a pleasure eternally new,
'Tis to gloat on the glaze and the mark
Of China that's ancient and blue.

Andrew Lang

26

We love the people we love for what they are.

Anonymous

Let me have wider feelings, more extended sympathies.
Let me share joy with all living things.

Anonymous

Joy is a feeling that comes from the
fulfillment of one's potential.

William Schutz

The secret of happiness is this: let your interests be as wide as
possible, and let your reactions to the things and persons that
interest you be as far as possible friendly rather than hostile.

Bertrand Russell

It is not right to vex ourselves at things,
For they care naught about us.
To the immortal gods and us, give joy.
Life must be reaped like the ripe ears of corn:
One man is born: another dies.
If gods care not for me and my children
There is a reason for it.
For the good is with me and the just.

Euripides

27

Of the beyond, I have no thought.
When you reduce this world to naught,
The other one may have its turn,
My joys come from this earth.

Johann Wolfgang von Goethe

Reason's whole pleasure
All the joys of sense
    Lie in these words — health, peace, competence
The soul's calm sunshine and heartfelt joy.

Alexander Pope

Joys too exquisite to last
    And yet more exquisite when past:
Bliss in possession will not last;
    Remembered joys are never past.
At once the fountain, stream, and sea,
    That were, they are, they yet shall be.

James Montgomery

Land of Heart's Desire,
Where beauty has no ebb, decay no
    flood,
But joy is wisdom, time an endless
    song.

William Butler Yeats

Sweets with sweets war not,
joy delights in joy.
William Shakespeare

Wrinkles should merely indicate where smiles have been.
Mark Twain

Ah happy days! too happy to endure!
    Such simple sports our plain forefathers knew;
No splendid vices glittered to allure
    Their joys were many, as their cares were few.
George Gordon, Lord Byron

Nothing contributes more to cheerfulness than the habit of looking at the good side of things. The good side is God's side of them.
W. B. Ullathorne

Let all thy joys be as the month of
    May,
And all thy days be as a marriage day:
Let sorrow, sickness, and a troubled
    mind
Be stranger to thee.
Francis Quarles

A merry heart doeth good like a medicine.

Proverbs 17:22

Hope elevates, and Joy brightens the crest.

John Milton

Joy redoubles
So that, whilst it lights upon my friend
It rebounds upon myself and
The brighter his candle burns —
The more easily will it light mine.

James South

The joy of a strong nature is cloudless.

Ouida

Joy is to see life steadily — to see it as a whole.

Sophocles

Joy of God

Fear not: for, behold,
I bring you good tidings of great joy,
which shall be to all people.

Luke 2:10

God is merely tuning the soul, as an instrument in this life. And these joys of the Christian are only the notes and chords that are sounded out in the preparation; preludes to the perfect harmony that shall flood the soul; forerunners of the perfected and rapturous joy that shall bless the soul, in that exceeding and eternal glory.

Herrick Johnson

God is glorified, not by our groans, but by our thanksgivings.

E. P. Whipple

31

To enjoy God is to feel spontaneously the delight in finding daily happiness in Him. All joy is gained from the contemplation of God's character or in His work or dispensation, whether it springs up in peace or self-approbation of our fellow creatures.

For God is the fountain of living waters, whence flows every stream of pleasure.

The enjoyment of God is our chief means of glorifying Him.

Timothy Dwight

Joy to the world! the Saviour reigns:
Let men their songs employ,
While fields and floods, rocks, hills and plains,
Repeat the sounding joy.

Isaac Watts

Be as I am, I consider the joys of the universe.
My will determines the ecstasy and meaning of each day.

Friedrich Wilhelm Nietzsche

In the beginning there was joy when God created
the heaven and the earth.

God saw every thing that he had made,
and, behold, it was very good.

Genesis 1:31

What will all earthly joys be,
compared to the promise:
Where I am, there ye may be also!

Anonymous

The joy of heaven will begin as soon as we attain the character
of heaven, and do its duties.

Theodore Parker

Judge not the Lord by feeble sense,
But trust Him for His grace;
Behind a frowning providence
He hides a smiling face.

His purposes will ripen fast,
Unfolding every hour:
The bud may have a bitter taste,
But sweet will be the flower.

William Cowper

Our actions are ours in respect of the free will which produces
them; but that they are also of God, in respect of His grace.
This enables our free will to produce them. God enables us to
do what is pleasing in His sight, by making us will to do even
what we might have been unwilling to do.

St. Augustine

We fall on one another's necks, more closely we
    embrace.
Not for ourselves, but for the Eternal family
    we live.
Man liveth not by self alone, but in his
    brother's face,
Each shall behold the Eternal Father and love and
    joy abound.
                                    William Blake

Shut fast the doors of woe,
In every place let flow
The streams of joy and peace.
                    Dietrich Bonhoeffer

God deigns His influence to infuse
Sweet refreshment, as the silent dews.
                    John Wesley

Joy is experienced in no small degree by good men. In the
future world, it will fill the minds of all glorified beings. They
behold their Maker.

The Lord is good, hence man rejoices in the Lord and finds
joy in the God of their Salvation. Life becomes a fullness of
joy and pleasure for evermore.
                    Timothy Dwight

Sometimes a Light surprises
    The Christian while he sings;
It is the Lord who rises
    With healing in his wings:
When comforts are declining,
    He grants the soul again
A season of clear shining,
    To cheer it after the rain.

Yet, God the same abiding,
    His praise shall tune my voice;
For while in him confiding,
    I cannot but rejoice.
        William Cowper

In spite of fear and pity, we are the happy living being, not as
individuals, but as the One Living Being with Whose pro-
creative joy we are blended.
        Charles Shaw

Honor and happiness unite
To make the Christian's name a praise
— a kingly character he bears
    No charge his priestly office knows
Unfading is the crown he wears
    His joys can never reach a close.
        William Cowper

Bliss is the enjoyment of God, the enjoyment of mankind, the enjoyment of things.

Ryder Smith

When we speak of joy, we do not speak of something we are after, but of something that will come to us when we are after God and duty.

Horace Bushnell

God cannot endure that unfestive, mirthless attitude of ours in which we eat our bread in sorrow, with pretentious, busy haste, or even with shame. Through our daily meals He is calling us to rejoice, to keep holiday in the midst of our working day.

Dietrich Bonhoeffer

The trouble with many men is that they have got just enough religion to make them miserable. If there is not joy in religion, you have got a leak in your religion.

Billy Sunday

Man finds his chief joy in the God who charms him, his soul is drawn toward Him infallibly, but of its own accord, by a motion perfectly free, spontaneous, love-impelled.

St. Augustine

. . . I caused the widow's heart to sing for joy.
I put on righteousness, and it clothed me: my judgment was as
a robe and diadem.
I was eyes to the blind, and feet was I to the lame.
I was a father to the poor: and the cause which I knew not I
searched out.

Job 29: 13-16

I believe in God — this is a fine, praiseworthy thing to say.
But to acknowledge God wherever and however he manifests
himself, that in truth is heavenly bliss on earth.

Johann Wilhelm von Goethe

Since happiness is nothing else but the enjoyment of the
Supreme Good, and the Supreme Good is above us, no one
can be happy who does not rise above himself.

St. Bonaventure

Perfect human joy is also worship, for it is ordered by God.

Friedrich Froebel

For the people who know the Bible and Tradition and the
complete history of humanity, Joy is the most infallible sign
of the presence of God.

Leon Bloy

37

Perfectly to will what God wills, to want what He wants, is
to have joy.

Meister Eckhart

Joy makes us giddy, dizzy.

Gothold Ephraim Lessing

When we serve with joy, we promote His honor and glory;
because we show that we do it with affection, and that all
we do is nothing compared to what we would wish to do.

Alphonsus Rodriguez

True joy will not spring up without ourselves.

Bishop Patrick

He who bends to himself a Joy
Doth the winged life destroy.
But he who kisses a Joy as it flies
Lives in Eternity's sunrise.

William Blake

Any man can again have the joy of his first meeting with God
if he will go back over the same road.

Roy L. Smith

As a countenance is made beautiful by the soul's shining through it, so the world is beautiful by the shining through it of God.

Friedrich Heinrich Jacobi

The contemplation of the divine Being, and the exercise of virtue, are in their own nature so far from excluding all gladness of heart, that they are perpetual sources of it.

Joseph Addison

A gay joy — our serene spirit is the source of all that is noble and good.

Johann von Schiller

There is but one way to tranquillity of mind and happiness, and that is to account no external things thine own, but to commit all to God.

Epictetus

'Tis much the doctrine of the times, that men should not please themselves, but deny themselves everything they take delight in; not look upon beauty, wear no good clothes, eat no good meat, etc., which seems the greatest accusation that can be upon the maker of all good things. If they be not to be used, why did God make them?

John Selden

Serenity comes to the man who lives with an unfaltering faith in an unfailing God. The person who lives with eternity in his heart will find a strange calm in his spirit.

Joseph R. Sizoo

We men are always complaining that our happy hours are so few and our sad hours so many, and yet it is we who are to blame. If we opened our hearts to enjoy the good that God offers us every day we should have strength enough to bear the evil in its turn when it does come.

Johann Wolfgang von Goethe

I am always content with that which happens, for I think that which God chooses is better than what I choose.

Epictetus